EMERGE!

Rise Up. Be Fearless.
Take Possession of Your Purpose!

Monica
Rise with purpose
everyday ! *[signature]*

EMERGE!

**Rise Up. Be Fearless.
Take Possession of Your Purpose!**

Kelley Johnson

SINCLAIRE SCOTT

MEDIA AND PUBLISHING

Emerge! Rise Up. Be Fearless.
Take Possession of Your Purpose!

Except where noted, all Scriptures are taken from the New Living Translation (NLT).

Cover Design: GermanCreative
Photography: R. Louise Photography
Editor: Morshe Araujo

ISBN 978-1-7329189-0-0

Sinclaire Scott Media and Publishing
c/o Kelley Johnson Enterprises LLC
1314 W. McDermott Drive
Suite 106-526
Allen, TX 75013
iamkelleyjohnson.com
Printed in the United States of America

TABLE OF CONTENTS

INTRODUCTION 1

PROPEL **5**

CHAPTER 1: A SHOT OF TRAGEDY 7

CHAPTER 2: YOU ARE A MASTERPIECE 21

REFINE **31**

CHAPTER 3: BLOOD, SWEAT, AND TEARS 33

CHAPTER 4: GET REAL SPIRITUALLY 47

CHAPTER 5: HAPPY IS THE ONE 61

IGNITE **71**

CHAPTER 6: LIKE A FIRE 73

CHAPTER 7: THE BIG REVEAL 83

PURSUE **95**

CHAPTER 8: PURSUE WITHOUT FORCE 97

CHAPTER 9: SURVIVAL GUIDE 109

FLOURISH **119**

CHAPTER 10: PURPOSE NOT PERFECTION 121

CHAPTER 11: CLOSING REMARKS 131

MEET THE AUTHOR 137

LET'S CONNECT! 139

REFERENCES 141

INTRODUCTION

I think I know why you picked up this book. I can relate to the longing – the burning desire to fulfill the void in your life. Sure, you could keep going through the normal, routine motions of life and let that nagging feeling simmer there a little longer or have you come to the realization, that now is the time? Is it like a distant drumbeat, softly calling you to ignore its rhythmic sounds no more?

God is calling you, and all you have to do is say, "Yes."

For now, your affirmative response applies to a relatively simple question.

Will you open your heart and mind to a greater capacity to allow the Holy Spirit to speak to you about your purpose?

Some of us are unsure about our purpose because it has not yet arrived in the package or format we are anticipating it to arrive in. Some of us may already have a hunch about what our calling is but are gripped by fear and unable to take the first step toward seeing our purpose manifest in our lives.

No matter where you are, will you suspend any preconceived notions you may have today about what a life purpose is or should be?

This book is about illuminating and demystifying the path to purpose. For too long in my own life, discovering my purpose seemed like a nebulous mystery. Cloaked in darkness, the path to finding purpose seemed unavailable.

While only the Father Himself knows the precise path, He is leading you right now. My prayer for this book is that it will help you understand some of the signs, phases and even processes you are likely to experience on your path to purpose.

From my personal experience and through watching the path to purpose unfold in the lives of clients I coach, I believe that there are five phases along the path to purpose.

By reading this book, you are now officially a Pathfinder. A Pathfinder is a woman on a mission. She relentlessly pursues a close relationship with Christ, which activates and sets in motion the path to purpose.

A Pathfinder is also astute and agile. She is confident that her mission is possible through Christ and is committed to studying His Word, transforming her thinking, letting go of the past and pruning dead habits and attitudes that limit what the Holy One wants to do in her life.

Pathfinders become familiar with the Life Purpose Map, which I share throughout this book. As a Pathfinder, you will learn how to use the Life Purpose Map to recognize where you are on your journey and what valuable lessons may be around the corner. The Life Purpose Map also helps you navigate rough terrain and the enemy's counter-attacks on her mission.

Recognizing where you are on the Life Purpose Map will hopefully reduce any anxiety or uncertainty you may feel. More than anything, as you pursue your purpose, you will need to develop an unwavering trust in the Almighty. Our faith and trust mature and develop based on our life experiences – it does not happen by osmosis!

So, get ready! He placed you in your mother's womb and has an assignment specifically designed for you to carry out. Your mission was established before the foundation of the world. It is a manifestation of God's Kingdom, here on earth.

As we begin, this journey, let's pray:

Gracious and Almighty Father, thank you that your Word says that you know the plans that you have for me. Plans to give me hope and a future [Jeremiah 29:11]. Thank you for these wonderful plans! Lord, I ask you to give me wisdom and discernment as I walk along the path to purpose. Please help me to be patient and steadfast. Don't let me give up or get tired of doing what is right. Lord, you didn't give up while you hung on the Cross, so I don't want to give up either! Please guide my footsteps and lead me in the way you would have me to go. Help me to hear your Voice and to know your Will for my life. I thank you, Lord, for hearing me. In Your Mighty Name, I pray. Amen.

Pathfinder Phase 1
Propel

Do not despise these small beginnings, for the LORD rejoices to see the work begin...

Zechariah 4:10

CHAPTER 1

A SHOT OF TRAGEDY

*For I know the plans I have for you," says the Lord.
"They are plans for good and not for disaster, to give you
a future and a hope. Jeremiah 29:11*

I was jolted from my sleep, awakened by his shouting and my mother's sobbing. I didn't hear the gunshot, but I saw the outcome. It was hard watching my mother holding a towel to her bleeding head. Along with my younger brother, I had been asleep in her bed that night. Trying to focus my eyes on the looming figure holding the gun in one hand, and gripping my mother tightly with the other, I will never forget my first thought at the sight before me. I was numb, and not really aware of my fear.

My eyes were locked on my mother. I remember what she was wearing. She had on a black and white striped knit halter-styled jumpsuit that she had sewn herself. She didn't sew very often, so this was special, at least to me. I was proud of what she had created. I remember seeing the small chunks of blood that had dripped and splattered down the front of her clothing. It was ruined! He ruined it!

In 1981, my stepfather shot my mother in the head. That one incident changed our family's life for many, many years. Thankfully, the bullet only skimmed my mother's skull - a miracle really; a true sign of God's grace and mercy. My stepfather also held my siblings and me at gunpoint that night. We were forced to stand against the wall as he paced the floor, brandishing his weapon. My mother lay on the couch across from us, holding a towel to her head, crying and praying feverishly. I am not even sure I cried. I could only focus on my mother. I can still see the scene in my mind as if I were a silent observer, as if it wasn't really happening to me.

Back then, the laws were different. The police didn't automatically arrest someone if there were obvious signs of domestic violence. My stepfather fled the scene once he realized the cops were coming, and my mother managed to get to the hospital.

I remember sitting in the cold waiting area of the emergency room, waiting for my mother to come out. As she numbly approached us, a coat haphazardly draped across her shoulders, her head was wrapped like a turban with stark white gauze. We didn't dare say a word to our mother. She had just gone through a traumatic ordeal and now, we had to leave the hospital with no safe place to go in the middle of the night. No social workers visited us. No hospital staff checked on our welfare. We had to figure it out by ourselves.

I recall my mother driving aimlessly after we left the hospital. I am sure she didn't know where to go. Physically and emotionally in pain, we rode in silence. At some point, the police pulled us over on this trip to nowhere. The police officer could obviously see my mother's bandaged head and asked her if she was okay. Sobbing deeply, she lied, and said, "Yes."

I was so angry that the police officer just walked away, leaving us. From the back seat, I wanted to scream at the top of my lungs, but I knew I couldn't. We ended up checking in to a dingy, smelly, and disgusting motel. Cheapest, nastiest place ever. The four of us squeezed into a queen-sized bed that night. I hated that place, convinced that it was rat-infested. I am sure my mother was still in pain and uncomfortable, as we all tried to fit in that tiny bed like a can of sardines.

For many years, I couldn't even drive down the highway and pass that place without a sneer on my face - rolling my eyes and wanting to avoid direct eye contact with the sight of it. That motel symbolized so much pain, and unfortunately, it still does to a degree.

We survived our one-night stay in the motel, and eventually went back "home," slowly piecing our life back together. Not long after, we moved out of the house with the bullet hole next to the front door. It seemed like we moved every few years, and every place we went, I carried shame, fear, and feelings of isolation. There were times we didn't know what we were going to eat for dinner. There were times the water was cut off because we couldn't afford to pay the bill. I was conditioned to keep all of the pain stuffed inside.

I was not a perfect kid by any means, but I often felt like it was my responsibility to help ease some of the weight and burden off my mother's shoulders. I loved school and worked hard. I sought perfection in my school work and activities, and felt wounded, if I somehow fell short of my self-inflicted standards of excellence.

I graduated high school with honors and went to college, where my past finally caught up with me. I suffered from depression and was not equipped to handle the tainted influences of campus life. Dealing with so much hardship as a kid and a lack of a positive father figure in my life, caused me to make stupid choices with my newfound freedom. After a couple of years, I was broke from mounting tuition debt that I had no way of paying. The stress put me in the hospital, which created even more debt, forcing me to drop out of college.

After moving back home, I landed a nice job at an advertising agency, but everything else in my life was in shambles. I had major debt, bad credit and a bad relationship. I was miserable, and I knew I was sinking deeper into turmoil. I eventually returned to the Lord. I was tired of bouncing on my bum, so I decided to bounce back to church. I began reading the Word and praying more. By this time, I was in my twenties and still wanted to live the foot-loose and fancy-free life, but I knew I wanted a better future.

Despite my bumps and bruises, the Lord gave me the strength to leave an unhealthy relationship once and for all. Not long after, God blessed me with a fantastic husband and set me on a wonderful career path without me even realizing it at the time. I went back to school part-time to finish my degree. My performance-driven tendencies were in full effect in my career and the Lord blessed me with great job opportunities where I worked hard to maximize them to the fullest potential. Over time, I worked my way up to the executive team of a Fortune 500 company, but I always had entrepreneurial aspirations since I was 16 years old. During my corporate career, I dabbled in a few side hustles that were profitable, but not feasible to maintain with my demanding corporate role, husband, and toddler on my hip. Following a layoff, the Lord brought me to a place where I became a full-time business owner.

As I look back over my life, I see that the Lord used all my life experiences – good, bad and ugly – to prepare me for each step of His Master Plan. He will also use all your life experiences to prepare you for His ultimate plan. Actually, He already is.

Ironically, I did not set out to write this book to tell you about my past. I would rather leave out all these personal details and instead focus on the appealing and exciting aspects about walking along the path to purpose, whistling and singing a tune as we go.

But I was reminded, maybe even compelled, to share a deeply personal example of how God will use the circumstances and experiences of our past to plant tiny purpose seeds for future use. Hindsight is often so much clearer than what we are able to see in the moment. What is most beautiful is when we can see that the Lord was there, even in our darkest most traumatic hours. Sure, our preference is to never suffer – never go through painful situations, but we have to trust that God knows what He's doing.

God's hand was there on that fateful night in 1981. He kept the bullet from penetrating my mother's skull. He kept my stepfather from shooting me and my siblings. The Lord was also with me during my stupid phase in college. When we are honest, we can look back and see God's grace, even when the outcome was far less than desirable. When we look deeper, we begin to see the purpose embedded within the moment. If we allow them, those nuggets become information and inspiration.

The Lord operates kind of like squirrels in that way. Squirrels work feverishly to bury nuts in the ground and inside trees to eat later. I believe God does that for us too. It all depends on our response to circumstances. And while we are inclined to want to throw out the bad nuts that are buried in our past, God can even use those too.

As Pathfinders, it is important to embrace, forgive, and accept all of who you are, including the painful life experiences that shaped and influenced you. Phase I is about creating deeper awareness about the impact our past has had on our lives, so that we can propel forward into purpose.

For me, it started with examining my childhood and acknowledging the pain and damage of it. Once I was able to acknowledge the source of my pain, I was able to see how God used some difficult circumstances to reveal His character and grace operating in my life.

From there, I began to see the Resilient Me emerge, tentatively at first, but there nonetheless. Despite difficult life experiences, it is never too late to move forward. While your pain and trauma are real, as a Pathfinder, I hope you also see yourself as a resilient child of God. When you allow the Holy Spirit to heal you from your past, God will use your experiences and the wisdom gained from them to propel you into purpose.

Unless a supernatural healing from your past comes from the Lord, please know that healing will likely be a long-term, if not life-long, endeavor. I often tell people that the healing process is like the layers of an onion.

Each time you allow the Lord to heal a layer of hurt and pain, it reveals new layers which also contain elements of the past tucked tightly between another layer. While I am not advocating that we should dwell in or permanently exist in our past, as new insights and awareness arise, we should embrace them, and ask the Lord to give us understanding.

I have had to come to terms with the impact of growing up without a relationship with my biological father. It created a gap in my sense of identity, and combined with an unsafe home life and stints with poverty, these aspects of my childhood all played an intricate role in shaping the woman I would later become. The woman I am now.

I know you picked up this book, hoping to find answers, and I think you will. The first answer may be to a question you didn't even know you had, and that is, "What does my past have to do with my purpose?"

While our past does not define us, God will often use it to set in motion a series of foundational building blocks for His future purpose.

And that, my Pathfinder, is what Phase I of the Path to Purpose is all about.

The quest for purpose and meaning can feel obscure, intangible and unobtainable at times. I want to help you recognize how God is already unfolding and outlining your purpose as you read this book. The challenge is not as much about *what* your purpose is but recognizing what may already be in front of you.

Compass Points

Reference these key learning points during your prayer and reflection time, and anytime you need a refresher about navigating your path to purpose.

1. God uses all our life experiences – good and bad – to prepare us for each step of His Master Plan. Don't try to edit what you think God can use.

2. Make an investment in yourself. Learn to embrace, forgive and accept all of who you are, including the painful life experiences that shaped and influenced you.

3. There is no time limit or expiration date for life transformation and healing. Don't believe the enemy's lies that you're too young or too old.

Coaching and Discovery Questions

1. What childhood dream or goal do you still hold on to today?

   _____

   _____

   _____

2. What are some of the significant life experiences that shaped you into the person you are today? Make a list and try to think holistically.

   _____

   _____

   _____

3. What painful aspects of your past or present life are affecting you today? How do these affect you?

   _____

   _____

   _____

Reflections

CHAPTER 2

YOU ARE A MASTERPIECE

For we are God's masterpiece. He has created us anew in Christ Jesus, so we can do the good things he planned for us long ago. Ephesians 2:10

Maybe your life story does not include any major traumatic events like mine, or maybe you have experienced even greater trauma and pain. Regardless of the setbacks, disappointments or hurt you have faced in the past, it is time to propel forward.

We have a job to do. It says so in Ephesians chapter two, and it is not just any job. It is a good job! That is exciting. Who doesn't want a *good* job?

Before we tackle understanding how we get to this good assignment the Word declares we will carry out, let's be honest. Do you view yourself as God's masterpiece? Or do you focus on your mistakes, the failed relationships or the ugly habits you cannot seem to stop doing?

Do you realize that He already planned for and made provision for you to do good things?

Many of us need to allow the Holy Spirit to reprogram the way we think about ourselves, otherwise, we will end up in a vicious cycle of self-doubt, self-recrimination, shame and frustration.

When confronted with feelings of insecurity, inadequacy or unworthiness, I like to remind myself of what is true – of what the Word of God says about me.

Negative self-talk or allowing negative people to hold prominent space in our lives is a sure-fire way to get derailed off the path to your purpose. Check-out Proverbs 18:21.

Pathfinder Tip: Pathfinders make it a habit to speak life and not death to themselves and those around them.

Get to Know God's Creation

Along the path to purpose, it's important to understand how we are God's masterpiece. For a moment, I want to challenge what you think you know about yourself.

Why? Because much of what we think about ourselves,

our gifts, strengths, and weaknesses, are so heavily influenced by what we have experienced in the past.

For example, let's say you grew up loving your mom's spaghetti. In fact, it was such a favorite meal, you learned to cook spaghetti just like your mom did and now, you serve it to your own family. You feel like it's one of your best dishes, and you get much satisfaction out of preparing it for your family.

One day, you and your family are invited to dinner at a neighbor's house. When you arrive, you discover that they are serving spaghetti. Secretly, your posture gets a little more erect and you silently snicker inside, because you know your family is going to wish that they were eating your spaghetti instead.

As everyone sits down to eat and begins to enjoy the meal, you recognize that your neighbor's spaghetti looks and tastes very different from your "world famous" spaghetti. You acknowledge to yourself that you like it, and then you glance around the table and hear your children already asking for a second serving of the neighbor's spaghetti!

How could they? Your spaghetti is their favorite, right?

Although a spaghetti dinner is a light-hearted scenario, it highlights how easily our past influences what we believe to be true, and in return, be dismissive about other ways of doing things.

On the path to purpose, we must get a very clear, honest, and objective view of ourselves, one free from our personal biases that have been formed, based on the life history tapes we play over and over again in our heads.

One of the ways to get clear about who you are and what makes you tick, is by understanding your personality and interests. Are you an introvert or an extrovert? Either way, He made you who you are for a reason.

While most of us are generally certain about whether we are an introvert or extrovert, we are only scratching the surface of our personality, if we stop there with our self-analysis.

Along your journey to purpose, I encourage you to periodically participate in a personality assessment if you can. Some workplaces provide personality assessments to their employees as part of leadership development programs. If you are a college student, most community colleges and universities provide free personality assessments like the Meyers-Briggs in the career services center.

There are literally hundreds of personality assessments out there, but some offer free or very low-cost versions online. Here are some of my favorite, budget-friendly personality assessments:

- 16personalities.com

- Howtofascinate.com

- Gallupstrengthscenter.com

Whatever you have access to, I highly recommend that you participate in a personality assessment as a simple way to objectively understand who you are.

If we are not careful, the Enemy may try to use our mistakes or painful past to thwart, derail, destroy or steal our purpose. But we know Satan is a liar, and his falsehood is defeated by the Truth, the Word of God. That's why I love the promise in Ephesians 2:10.

God already knows how He wants to use you. What's key is that we not get consumed by the mere pursuit of our purpose. We have to pursue Christ who reveals our purpose. We will talk more about that later in Chapter 8. For now, I want you to understand that there are no mistakes or hurts that God cannot use.

Compass Points

Key learning and reflection points from this chapter.

1. Negative self-talk or allowing negative people to hold prominent space in our lives is a sure-fire way to get derailed off the path to your purpose.

2. Own who God made you to be, but don't let that be an excuse to never grow, stretch, change, and eliminate negative or harmful habits, thoughts, and behaviors.

3. Pursue a deep and intimate relationship with Christ. He is our first priority, not our "purpose."

Coaching and Discovery Questions

1. What are some things you are passionate about?

    _____

    _____

    _____

2. What are some things that totally disinterest you?

    _____

    _____

    _____

3. What negative self-talk are you using that is contrary
    to what Scripture says about you?

    _____

    _____

    _____

4. Who in your inner circle (friends, family, coworkers, church members, etc.) could you make it a habit to speak words of life to?

_____

_____

_____

Reflections

_____

_____

_____

_____

_____

_____

_____

_____

_____

_____

_____

Pathfinder Phase 2

Refine

He cuts off every branch of
mine that doesn't produce
fruit, and he prunes the
branches that do bear fruit
so they will produce
even more.

John 15:2

CHAPTER 3

BLOOD, SWEAT, AND TEARS

This means that anyone who belongs to Christ has become a new person. The old life is gone; a new life has begun!

2 Corinthians 5:17

Pathfinders are more precious than rubies or gold. We are difference makers. The ones who are willing to make sacrifices and changes in our lives now, so that we will positively impact generations to come. But even gemstones and precious metals must go through a process in order to achieve their highest value. We are no different.

To live a life of purpose, we will go through a refining process. Quite frankly, as Christ Followers, refinement is a perpetual way of life, but there will be periods of intensity along the path to purpose.

Simply put, to refine means to make pure. Our default sin nature and the fallen state of our world means that to become more Christ-like, we will have to submit to the Lord's refining and pruning process.

To be honest, this aspect of the Pathfinder's trek will likely be rough and uncomfortable terrain. This is also the point on the journey when some will be tempted to give up, turn around and return to their comfort zone. Refining begins by acknowledging and accepting that we need to change. It will likely involve some level of the following:

- Surrendering our preconceived notions, plans, and timelines.

- Adjusting our lifestyle, entertainment, and social habits or practices.

- Gut-checking our emotions, attitudes, and mind-sets with the Word of God.

- Being open to accountability.

In I Corinthians 15:31, the Apostle Paul said that he dies daily, and Jesus himself instructed us to deny ourselves and take up the cross daily to follow Him (Luke 9:23). As a Pathfinder, you must hold nothing sacred or off-limits about yourself on this journey. Every fiber of your being will be stretched and challenged. Things that were normally easy for you, may no longer be.

In my personal experience and in walking this journey with other women, I have seen time and again, how the Lord will begin to dramatically shift our lives all for the sake of refining. In many cases, those shifts will look and feel like major life disruptions. Our natural instinct is to resist disruption, whether it is an end to a relationship, a layoff, illness or geographic relocation. When life disruptions occur, pray and ask the Lord to help you to see what He wants to show you through this experience.

Getting Stuff Done

Pathfinders usually fall into two categories: those who do all they can to make things happen and those who are content to let things unfold more naturally. The first type of Pathfinder, the Trailblazer, knows her strengths and is adept at using them to achieve what she wants. She has faced some obstacles in the past, but through sheer grit and grace, she has hurdled some high mountains to achieve many of her goals.

On the other hand, the Analyzer has also created a nice life but is conservative, analytical and makes careful calculations before she makes a major move. Like her counterpart, she has overcome some major obstacles in life, and attributes her success to grace and prudence.

There will come a time on the path to purpose when your usual tactics and methods you use to get stuff done will no longer work. As you mature spiritually, God will begin to remove the familiar crutches He previously allowed when we were spiritual younglings. Through His infinite wisdom and sovereignty, I believe when we first begin to walk with Him, He will tolerate or allow a certain amount of flesh still being the lead dog in your life. But woe to those of us whom He leaves there!

For Pathfinders who decide to take up their cross daily, there will come a point on the path when the Lord flips a switch. Unfortunately, I don't think He will likely tell you when it will happen either. That's why I want to warn you now. I want you to be able to recognize this important lesson when it begins.

For Analyzers, you will likely be challenged to step out boldly and courageously to do something you normally wouldn't. God will require you to confront, act, speak up or call-out in a way that flies in the face of self-preserving prudence and caution.

Trailblazers beware! Your normal approach to being the take-charge "Fixer" will not work. In the past, you may have been able to burp the baby, close the deal and wear six-inch stilettos all at the same time, but God will say no more! Go sit down and wait until I tell you to move.

This is why I cannot stress enough the importance of a close, personal relationship with the Lord, made real through daily Scripture reading and prayer. Communion with the Holy Spirit is the only way you will be able to recognize when Jesus turns the light on to His way of getting things done.

Regardless of your Pathfinder style, one pitfall we all need to avoid is procrastination. Procrastination is a stealthy robber who sneaks into our lives and delays or deters our ability to live a fulfilling life. We all have moments or seasons when we procrastinate, but if you find that you consistently delay addressing certain areas or tasks in your life, it's time to take the proverbial bull by the horns and deal with it.

In my own life, and that of my coaching clients, I find that chronic or systemic procrastination is often rooted in fear, unbelief, good old-fashioned bad habits or some combination of all three. Fear of failure and feelings of unworthiness stifle forward movement. When our knowledge of Scripture is limited, our belief in what God says about us will likely be low as well. Self-defeating habits like over-eating and over-spending can delay or stall our efforts to be healthy and good stewards of the resources the Lord has provided. Even fear of being the "mean girl" by setting healthy boundaries and expectations in our relationships can halt or suspend God bringing healing and restoration to our families and friendships.

When our son was in high school, we had to address some ungodly behavior that had been going on for a while. Generally speaking, he was a very good kid. His teachers loved him and he did well in school, but at home, there were times when he was blatantly disrespectful towards me and my husband, and more importantly, the Lord.

One day, we busted him right before he was set to leave on a student trip that had been in the works for months. My husband and I were deeply hurt by his behavior, and we made the extremely difficult decision to not allow him to go on the trip. Making that decision felt like my heart had been ripped from my chest and broken into a million pieces, even though I knew it was the right thing to do.

Holding staunchly to our standards sent a big message to our son, and after that day, a slow progression towards greater respect and obedience began. I wish I could say things completely turned around overnight, but they didn't. However, looking back, I can only imagine where our family would be if we had delayed or avoided addressing the issue.

Procrastination, in any form and in any area of our lives, will hold us hostage from walking in our purpose. To overcome it, we must replace the lies of the enemy with the Truth of God's Word. We also have to create a no-excuses environment of accountability and transparency to put procrastination in the corner and leave it there. Secrecy and masking issues or pretending everything is fine, will get you nowhere fast. I want to encourage you to ask the Lord to send you godly, trustworthy and loving friends who will speak the truth in love and support your efforts to break-free from procrastination and self-sabotaging habits.

Reconciling the Past With the Present

During the refining process, it is so important to invest the time to do the hard work. Speed is not the goal here. We have to roll up our sleeves and be open to the promptings of the Holy Spirit and what He is trying to show us.

During this journey, we need to take a critical look at what aspects of our past are coming forward with us in the present. If we are in a hurry to walk in our purpose, we may be reluctant to look at our past, especially the painful experiences. But it is those very painful and tender wounds that we need to allow the Holy Spirit to heal and transform.

Why is it important to deal with the past? Because it will likely inform our future, and there are some things God can't do in our lives until we have healed from our past on a deeper level. Our childhood and adult experiences are all part of God's equation when He uses you in His Kingdom. Walking in purpose means you have a degree of understanding about who and how God made you, and what He wants you to do to carry out His plans. Our past is an aspect of who we are, and likely what contributed, in part, to you becoming a Trailblazer or Analyzer. Be sure to embrace all of who you are on this journey.

Many of us really struggle with looking back at the past, and while we should not take up permanent residence there, it should also not be ignored or swept under the proverbial rug. There can be some golden nuggets from our past that show up in new ways in the future.

Oprah Winfrey once coined the phrase, "Aha moment." She explained that you can't have an "aha moment" unless you already knew something. She defined an "aha moment," as a remembering of what you already knew articulated in a way that resonates with your own truth.

While Oprah may get credit for coining this catchy phrase, look at John 14:26:

"But when the Father sends the Advocate as my representative— that is, the Holy Spirit—he will teach you everything and will remind you of everything I have told you."

Pathfinder Tip: When the Holy Spirit brings something to your remembrance or attention, write it down. It may be a significant mile marker on your path to purpose.

One pretty significant "aha moment" happened during a performance review at work, early in my career. I had only been at this organization for about a year, so this was my first performance review at this company. The performance conversation was moving along smoothly, but then the conversation shifted when my boss started talking about my interpersonal communication skills. He stammered a bit and struggled to find the right words to say, and then he blurted out, "You're like a piece of granite."

Stunned, I sat there silently trying to process the comment and feedback. I really didn't understand where he was coming from. I knew his statement wasn't good, but I didn't understand what he meant. Since I'm sure a dazed and confused look was written all over my face, my manager went on to say that I tended to keep people at a distance and that I'm hard to get to know on a personal level. In other words, I was all business.

While I tried to preserve the remnants of my dignity as I left the meeting, internally, I was fuming inside. My first reaction was, "How dare he say that about me!"

Eventually, my temper cooled, and I began to question why I was coming across that way at work. Once I was able to objectively consider what he said, I realized that the answer to my question was connected to my past.

As a kid, there were times when we were not sure how we

were going to eat and from those experiences, I learned to hide my struggles by disconnecting from people. We were raised not to ask for help, and to cover up the pain and the hurt, I learned that you couldn't be an open book about your feelings – especially to outsiders.

And so, my 'aha moment,' was a realization that even as an adult, I was bringing my childhood into my career. I knew I had a decision to make. I had to overcome my fears about being more open and relatable to people. It wasn't an overnight flip-the-light-switch experience. It was one that I had to really work through because it came from years and years of conditioning.

Whether at work, in our relationships or even personal habits, many of our personality traits are heavily influenced by our past. Thankfully, the Lord can restore what was lost or stolen from us (Joel 2:25). There is nothing too difficult for Him!

Compass Points

Key learning and reflection points from this chapter.

1. The refining process is necessary. It begins by acknowledging and accepting that we need to change in order to reflect more of His character.

2. Consider your default style of how you get things done and know that the Lord may cause you to flip the script at times. The personality style is not what is important; it's about being fully submitted to His ways.

3. When "aha moments" arise, recognize that they are a gift from the Holy Spirit. Be willing to seek greater understanding and take action.

Coaching and Discovery Questions

1. Which type of Pathfinder, Trailblazer or Analyzer, do you resonate with the most and why?

_____

_____

_____

2. Why do you think the Lord will sometimes cancel our usual tactics for getting things done?

_____

_____

_____

3. What part of your past is impacting your present right now?

_____

_____

_____

Reflections

_____

_____

_____

_____

_____

_____

_____

_____

_____

_____

_____

_____

CHAPTER 4

GET REAL SPIRITUALLY

You can make many plans, but the Lord's purpose will prevail. Proverbs 19:21

I'm a big fan of coconut oil. It tastes great in recipes and feels luscious on my hair and skin. On grocery store shelves, you usually see a couple of varieties of coconut oil. Some say refined and others say unrefined. As you now know, refining means to filter and remove impurities; to make purer. Through refinement, the most desired attributes are often able to emerge, to spring forth.

As we have already started learning to know our life's purpose, we must allow the Lord to refine us. The degree to which we are willing to bend our will to align to His will determine how much of our old self He is able to refine in us. Allowing the Lord to filter out the qualities that will not serve us as He moves us toward purpose is essential. It is through God's refinement process that we are led to a greater level of spiritual authenticity.

What is spiritual authenticity?

Spiritual authenticity is integrating your faith into every area of your life. The degree to which you are spiritually authentic depends on three concepts.

1. How your faith in Christ informs your decisions.

2. How your relationship with Christ is relevant in all areas of your life.

3. How your walk with Christ is consistently practiced and nurtured.

When we are spiritually authentic, our faith in Christ informs everything we do. Our decision-making criteria are based on Scripture, prayer, and fasting. No aspect of our life is untouched by the hand of God. We welcome and invite Him to guide our relationships, our habits, our time, our everything.

Do you have a room, drawer or closet in your house you would never want guests to see? You know, the junky, catch-all space that you've been meaning to declutter. When we are spiritually authentic, there are no "junky closets" that we avoid, allowing God to see and touch everything, which is surrendered to Him no matter how dysfunctional or messy. We can't horde a few areas of our lives while only leaving Him the breadcrumbs. We are students of the Word and are hungry for it to infuse all the nooks and crannies of who we are.

Being spiritually authentic does not mean we have perfect faith or a perfect relationship with the Lord. It just means our point of reference for all things is Christ. As an adopted daughter or son of God through Christ, your faith is relevant to every area of your life. Many times, we think of faith in terms of our level of belief in something. For those of us who are striving to be spiritually authentic, it means the Lord and our faith in Him is relevant in all that we do.

How often does Christ enter your conversations with friends or family members?

We prioritize and make room for the people and things that are most important to us. If we hold God dear to our heart, He will be near our heart. We will desire to be in His presence as often as possible. Our ultimate #relationship-goals will be for Christ.

Finally, spiritual authenticity is about living a life of faith that is not confined to being exercised or practiced only on Sundays. Some of us may think about our relationship with the Lord as something we do on Sundays.

Many Christians, have a Sunday to Monday divide, meaning the person they are Monday through Saturday can sometimes be a variation of the person who shows up to church. So, being spiritually authentic is really about a life of congruency. Your relationship with the Lord is congruent with who you are and who you want to be.

There are 168 hours in a seven-day week. If the average church service is approximately an hour and a half, we are barely giving the Lord ten percent of our time if we limit our relationship to Sundays only.

Would we only give our jobs or businesses ten percent of our time and focus? Probably not.

For some of us, living a life of spiritual consistency may require us to really examine what we believe. If you have been disappointed by a church leader or member, it can sometimes taint our beliefs or alter how we practice our faith.

I want to encourage you today to not let the shortcomings of people, even those who are in religious leadership, get you out of your true game. Our eyes have to stay focused on the prize of Jesus Christ. Unfortunately, people will always disappoint us - even those who have gone to seminary and have been pastors for thirty years. When we allow church-related disappointments to hinder our walk with the Lord, we are actually doing what scripture calls focusing on the stick in someone else's eye instead of the beam in our own eye (Matthew 7:5).

If we are focused more on the different ways people have disappointed us, then we are probably not considering the different ways we have disappointed other people. Can any of us honestly say that we have never disappointed someone? It's unlikely that we haven't and it's very likely that we will disappoint someone in the future.

Sadly, there are people who misuse the Word of God and they manipulate what scripture says in order to justify their own behaviors. That's why we must be students of the Word to not be deceived, confused, or disappointed when "church folks" let us down.

So, to recap, spiritual authenticity is about your faith informing everything you do, your faith being relevant to every area of your life and living a life of faith that is congruent on a day-to-day basis. I believe that it is through spiritual authenticity that we thrive in life.

Some people may focus on success or achievement, but I like to focus on *thriving*.

There is a subtle distinction between success and thriving. Unfortunately, in our society, I feel as if the word *success* has a little excess baggage with it. Many people have compromised values, relationships, and even health for the sake of being successful. That's why I try to emphasize a thriving life. Thriving includes elements of how the world defines success, but to thrive means that we flourish in a way that aligns with the Word of God and the Character of God.

As we grow in spiritual authenticity, we blossom and prosper in a way that is authentic to who God created us to be in this world. Inherently the Lord is a God of balance, rest and wellbeing. We can have those things when we live surrendered to Him.

We know Scripture tells us that we should seek first the Kingdom of God and his righteousness and that everything else will be added unto us (Matthew 6:33). Scripture also tells us that if we delight ourselves in the Lord, He will give us the desires of our heart (Psalms 37:4).

Through these passages of Scripture, we see the significance of a God-first, spiritually authentic view of life. We see an appreciation and belief that when we focus on God first, the rest of our life will fall into place. And while things will fall into place, know that it will not always be a beautiful and carefree process or experience. Scripture tells us that we will face trials and tribulations, but we must keep our focus on the Lord so that we can have peace during those difficult seasons in our lives.

So why is spiritual authenticity important?

First and foremost- it will create a life that is submitted to the purposes of God. But there are added benefits. When we are living a spiritually authentic life, we have more energy. We focus on our health. We have greater levels of peace, resilience, purpose, and finally a legacy. Millions of Americans are burned out, constantly tired, battling insomnia, anxiety disorders, and depression. When we don't put Christ first in our life, we can miss out on opportunities to establish healthy boundaries that protect our wellbeing, our energy levels, and our health. We know that

God himself rested on the seventh day after He created the world.

Who are we not to rest? When we're spiritually authentic, we view our bodies as God's Temple and however flawed we may think they are, we recognize that our bodies should be treated as important and well taken care of.

Our health can improve as we ask the Lord to guide us into the right diet and exercise habits, and even seeking Him and His strength to help us to make consistently better health choices. We often quote the scripture that God will keep us in perfect peace if our mind stays focused on Him (Isaiah 26:3).

This verse is catchy and sounds good to memorize and quote, but do we really have the peace of God? With certainty, it can be a challenge to maintain our peace, but Scripture gives us a promise in that verse that is exciting. The peace of God gives us the ability to keep moving forward, even during some of the most difficult challenges in life. We develop resilience which is important as we face situations that can throw us for a loop.

We can rejoice, too, when we run into problems and trials, for we know that they help us develop endurance. And endurance develops strength of character, and character strengthens our confident hope of salvation. And this hope will not lead to disappointment. For we know how dearly God loves us because he has given us the Holy Spirit to fill our hearts with his love. Romans 5:3-5

This passage of Scripture truly summarizes the refining process on our path to purpose. If we allow ourselves to go through God's refining process, we will develop a confident hope in Him. Refining is how we come to understand our purpose. The refining road toward spiritual authenticity is the path toward leaving a legacy or our mark on our families and communities. We can either choose to be intentional about our legacy or it can be one that is formed haphazardly. If you're reading this book, I think you want to be intentional about the legacy that you leave.

Through spiritual authenticity, you can discover your life's purpose and your legacy will be established. Your legacy will be clear, and you can look toward heaven without any regrets when that day comes.

Until then, I want you to pray and consider what areas of your life may not be fully surrendered to Christ. Don't bypass or try to avoid the refining process. It is an essential part of your path to purpose. There is richness in the journey, and there are no shortcuts. The journey to your purpose is just as important as actually walking in your purpose. If we try to take the easy road, we can short-circuit the process and delay learning invaluable lessons from life experiences.

I find that many of us try to focus exclusively on what we believe is the "ultimate prize" which is walking in our purpose. When we have such a narrow vision or try to follow a formulaic, mechanical process to know our purpose, we miss the life lessons, refinement and blessings God wants to give us along the way.

Compass Points

Key learning and reflection points from this chapter.

1. When we are spiritually authentic, our faith in Christ informs everything we do.

2. Your faith in Christ is relevant to every area of your life. Avoid separation of church and state or compartmentalizing certain areas of your life away from God's guidance and influence.

3. The journey to your purpose is just as important as actually walking in your purpose. This is not the time to take the short cut.

Coaching and Discovery Questions

1. Are faith and Scripture informing every area of your life? What areas of your life might be missing a Biblical view right now?

   _____

   _____

   _____

2. What parts of your life are being kept in the 'junk drawer' away from the Lord?

   _____

   _____

   _____

3. How can you improve the congruency of your relationship with Christ through better time management?

   _____

   _____

   _____

Reflections

CHAPTER 5

HAPPY IS THE ONE

*Joyful are people of integrity, who follow the instructions
of the Lord. Psalms 119:1*

P athfinders pursue purpose because there is an inherent desire to live a fulfilling, and dare I say it, a "happy" life. As Christians, we know that there is a distinct difference between happiness and joy. There is nothing wrong with experiencing happiness, and hopefully, you will enjoy many moments of pure bliss. But the reality is, happiness is a short-term emotion that requires certain conditions to exist. There are specific qualifiers before we can experience happiness.

Fortunately, happiness has a cousin named *joy*. Joy has some sustaining power and is one of the fruits of the Holy Spirit. While joy can feel like happiness at times, true joy, that comes from the Lord, is less conditional. Spiritual joy is a learned behavior and state of being. You know it must be good when the enemy works so hard to try to steal it from you.

Those of us on the path to purpose understand that a great job is like happiness. In the grand scheme, even the best job is temporary and the qualities that make it a great job can change like a swift shift of the wind.

Our calling, on the other hand, is like joy. It reaches far beyond even the span of time we can see, and its impact on our lives and those around us is less dependent upon a specific set of criteria being perfectly in place.

Without a doubt, employment and business ownership are very necessary means of earning an income. My challenge to you is to look beyond the comfortable 9-to-5 job with a nice 401k plan, because deep down, Pathfinders can never seem to escape the perpetual question of, "Is there more to life than this?"

The Aleph Principle

Psalms 119, the longest chapter in the entire Bible, sheds amazing light on the spectacular connection between living a fulfilling, purpose-driven life and entwining it with our relationship with the Lord.

Before we get into the details, let me familiarize you with Psalms 119 because it is truly unique. Although David is the primary author of the Psalms, according to some biblical commentary, the writer of Psalms 119 is unknown. The structure of this chapter is also distinctive. It is a Hebrew acrostic poem consisting of 22 stanzas – one for each letter of the Hebrew alphabet. Each stanza contains eight verses and each verse begins with that letter of the Hebrew alphabet.

Psalms 119 is chock full of deep and complex meaning and can be taxing to read in one sitting. However, the first stanza illuminates what the journey to a purposeful life looks like. Read Psalms 119:1-8.

The first letter of the Hebrew alphabet is aleph, pronounced, /ah-lef/, and parallels the very familiar Greek word, *alpha*. Aleph has several meanings, including steer, power, beginning, authority, and strength (Benner, 2018). Within the first eight verses of Psalms 119, we find a connection to power and strength that comes from following Christ in all areas of life. A study of Bible commentary provides wonderful insight about the foundational tenets of what I call, the Aleph Principles (Benson, 2018).

1. A joyful life comes from a life of integrity and keeping God's commandments.

2. To pursue Christ means to follow His path in every area of our lives.

3. Those whose hearts and lives agree with their profession of faith are blessed.

4. Our lives must be ordered and arranged according to the rule of God's Word.

5. In mind and heart, carefully and diligently observe his law, standards or code.

6. God's presence and favor is the number one pursuit, and fervent attention is given to avoiding known sin.

7. Life decisions are based on the paths which God has prescribed to them.

Living and breathing the principles found within Aleph is what we must press toward! This is the high calling of Jesus! (Philippians 3:14)

We know that God is a rewarder of those who diligently seek Him (Hebrews 11:6). That reward is often attributed to some type of material or monetary gain, but some of the most beautiful rewards are joy, peace, and satisfaction from knowing you are doing what He called you to do.

Applying the Aleph Principles to your life is a lifetime experience. It literally never stops, and I think it is a critical aspect of how the Lord prepares us for our purpose.

Previously, I mentioned that we should not rush the refining process. If we look at the life of Jesus, we can see how much emphasis God places on preparation. Jesus' refining and preparation phase lasted thirty years. His "official" ministry lasted three years. Esther was selected to be Queen, but her beautification and preparation phase lasted twelve months – a whole year of beauty treatments! (I want those kinds of spa days!)

As a young boy, Joseph was given dreams and visions about his future, but he did not walk into his purpose until after years and years of extreme hardship. And while the Bible does not tell us the exact number of years it took Noah to build the ark, some theologians and archeologists suggest that it was built over a span of seventy years.

The bottom line is, we must embrace <u>all</u> the journey. There are no shortcuts on the path to purpose. Oprah Winfrey said, "No experience is ever wasted. Everything has meaning," and I agree.

Biblically, we can see that the Lord has never wasted an experience for those who follow Him. So, never feel like it is too late or too soon to walk in purpose. God's time is the perfect time.

Compass Points

Key learning and reflection points from this chapter.

1. Spiritual joy is a learned behavior and state of being. It is not contingent on everything being perfect in our lives.

2. Psalms 119 illustrates the connection between living a fulfilling, purpose-driven life and entwining it with our relationship with the Lord.

3. The Lord is multi-dimensional and multi-functional. Through Him, no life experience is ever futile or without merit and value.

Coaching and Discovery Questions

1. Which tenets of the Aleph principles stand out the most to you and why?

   _____

   _____

   _____

2. As you look back over your life, what experiences, good and bad, have been foundational in shaping you into the person you are today?

   _____

   _____

   _____

3. What life experiences have you perhaps dismissed up until now, that the Lord is revealing to you were actually for your good?

   _____

   _____

   _____

Reflections

_____

_____

_____

_____

_____

_____

_____

_____

_____

_____

_____

_____

Pathfinder Phase 3

Ignite

In the same way, let your good deeds shine out for all to see so that everyone will praise your heavenly Father.

Matthew 5:16

CHAPTER 6

LIKE A FIRE

But if I say I'll never mention the LORD or speak in his name, his word burns in my heart like a fire. It's like a fire in my bones! I am worn out trying to hold it in! I can't do it!" Jeremiah 20:9

O n the path to purpose, every Pathfinder will come to a point on the trail where a fire will ignite within her. This moment is so profound, yet unique to each woman.

When purpose ignites, it is a culmination of every life experience, every gift, and talent coming together with a force like no other. It is unexplainable yet undeniable.

Many women wonder, "How will I know when I have found my purpose?" Trust me, you will know, but you may have a few false starts before you know with certainty.

When I was pregnant with both children, I was so ready to meet my new little bundles of joy and get my body back to one owner, that my wishful thinking and impatience led me to the hospital before it was really time.

On more than one occasion, the doctor or nurse would examine me and sheepishly, yet knowingly smile, and say, "Sorry, you are not in labor yet."

Oh! Those were *not* the words I wanted to hear at that moment! Surely, I was ready to have the baby, I thought each time. But once actual labor finally came, I quickly recognized the stark contrast between false labor and the real delivery time.

While the path to purpose is not necessarily linear, it is perfectly designed by the Father for you. Up until this point, we have mostly focused on the inner workings of who God created you to be and how He got you here, to this moment in time.

Before we go further, let's unlock some of the foundational principles about purpose. What it is and Biblical examples of how God revealed purpose in others' lives.

What is Purpose?

Purpose and calling are often used interchangeably in the English language. In modern times, there has been a huge shift from what the Bible indicates as a correlation between our work profession and our spiritual life.

For example, the Latin root for *vocation* means calling. While we use the word vocation almost exclusively now to refer to career, trade or industry, its original meaning implies purpose.

A simple definition of purpose is the reason why something exists. What I like about the word purpose, is that it has an underlying message of fortitude, determination, and commitment to a cause or mission.

In Hebrew, the original language for the Old Testament, the word used to describe *work* is *avodah*, and it first appears in Genesis chapter two. In Hebrew, *avodah* has three meanings: work, worship, and service.

Biblical References to Avodah

1. As *work*, it occurs forty-two times in the King James Version. See Exodus 39:42, 2 Chronicles 34:13 and Psalms 104:23.

2. As worship, avodah is used five times. See Joshua 24:14; Ezekiel 20:40 and Exodus 3:12.

3. As *service*, it is used eighty-nine times in the King James Version. See Exodus 35:21, Numbers 4:4 and 2 Chronicles 31:2.

In the King James Version, *work* is referenced in Scripture three hundred seventy-nine times and *works* are mentioned two hundred twenty-four times.

The bottom line is that the work we do everyday matters to God. Scripture tells us that we were made in God's image. God Himself worked for six days creating the universe. Soon after God created man, He instructs man and woman to, "Be fruitful and multiply." (Genesis 1:28)

We all love that Scripture because we tend to focus on that verse being our free pass to the wonderful pleasures of procreation; however, the verse does not stop there.

God further instructs man and woman to govern the earth and reign over all creatures. To govern is to manage, create structure, processes, and systems. So, even in the very first chapter of the Bible, God does not limit the scope of work to agricultural pursuits which would have been the primary form of work during the time.

There are more scriptures in the Bible about money and possessions than there are scriptures about prayer. Money and possessions are the results or byproducts of working. In sixteen of the thirty-eight parables Jesus used when teaching, He referred to money or possessions. You may be wondering, why are we talking about money and possessions in a book about calling and purpose?

Well, for many of us, our calling will be associated with what we do on a daily basis in the form of our career or our service to others. God knows that in order to earn money, in order to obtain possessions, we have to work. The Bible is clear that if a man doesn't work, he doesn't eat (2 Thessalonians 3:10). And while most of us tend to think of a calling or purpose as reserved for the holy and sacred, I think the Scriptures' references to money and possessions tell us that there's a level of practicality and everydayness in our purpose.

If you are an artist, you can operate in your calling as an artist. We can walk in purpose as a sanitation worker, a fast-food restaurant worker, an executive at a Fortune 100 organization, or a CEO for a nonprofit. We all earn a living in a variety of ways. Sometimes, we will operate in our calling and purpose in our everyday work.

I think the tendency is for most of us to think that once we discover our calling, we must change or shift our careers for God's plan to fully manifest. While that may happen, God is not isolated to working in only one way. As Pathfinders, we must first address any preconceived notions or expectations of what it will look like to walk in your purpose.

Your career field may or may not change. I believe that God wants us to find a way to bring Him glory and draw others to him in whatever work we do. Whether we are a college student or a CEO, God wants us to help bring others to Him. We should all be actively seeking ways to draw others to Christ and bring Him glory through the work that we perform with our hands.

I think the challenge as Christians is that we spend so much of our lives leaving God out of our careers and out of our day-to-day routine. We spend so much time isolating or confining Christ to Sunday and perhaps a few minutes here or there during our devotional reading time.

God wants to be in the middle of everything that we do: every interaction in the grocery store, every interaction serving in the PTA. God wants to be involved with us, and I think that's a practical way to look at what it means to walk by faith and by the Holy Spirit.

We can't be open to the promptings of the Lord if we're not walking by faith and walking by the spirit. This goes back to living congruently and being spiritually authentic. Congruency is not just about integrating your faith into your career. Congruency is about being connected with the Lord, being congruent with his Spirit, and the more we allow him to be infused in our lives, the more we will understand our path to purpose.

Compass Points

Key learning and reflection points from this chapter.

1. The path to purpose is not linear, but it is perfectly designed by the Father for you.

2. There is an intimate and supernatural connection between the work we do to earn a living, how we serve others and how we worship Christ.

3. The Lord wants to be in the middle of everything that we do. He is not a distant and untouchable God. He is active and always present.

Coaching and Discovery Questions

1. What are your views about integrating your faith into your current work?

   _____

   _____

   _____

2. What feels easy and challenging about living a congruent life?

   _____

   _____

   _____

3. Do you feel your current work is "just a job" or is it a "vocation or calling?" Why?

   _____

   _____

   _____

Reflections

_____

_____

_____

_____

_____

_____

_____

_____

_____

_____

_____

_____

CHAPTER 7

THE BIG REVEAL

But on the judgment day, fire will reveal what kind of work each builder has done. The fire will show if a person's work has any value. 1 Corinthians 3:13

O h boy, am I a huge HGTV junkie. I love the anticipation of the big reveal – the moment when the couple decides which house they will buy (even though we know they have already purchased it) – or the moment when the family finally gets to see the completed renovation.

For those few seconds of waiting for the big reveal, I am practically holding my breath. When my husband and I watch HGTV together (which is often), we always vote on which house we think the people will choose and celebrate when we get it right.

When a Pathfinder's purpose ignites within, it's like a big reveal. It is a momentous occasion in your life, worthy of recording, celebrating and documenting. While the formula for the big reveal on HGTV is routine, God's methods for uncovering our purpose are unique and special for each of us.

Thankfully, we have Scripture to help us recognize some of the ways God has ignited purpose in others. We will look at Biblical examples of the defining moments when a person gained significant awareness about how God wants to use them.

Purpose Defining Moments

Because God is, well God, He is not confined to a method, system or formula. Many Pathfinders will question or be concerned about whether they will be able to recognize their divine assignment when the time comes. Some of you may even be wondering if you have already missed the sign.

Let's look at Scripture for an indication of how purpose may be revealed for modern Pathfinders.

The Burning Bush

In Exodus 3, Moses is summoned by a burning bush into the Presence of God, where he is given a direct assignment from the Lord. Wouldn't it be amazing if we all experienced a burning bush moment to learn our purpose? While this may seem like the absolute easiest way to identify your purpose, if we look at the background of Moses' life up until this moment, we will notice that God used life experiences to refine and develop him for this moment. Even so, Moses was reluctant to accept his assignment and struggled with feelings of unworthiness. Even when our calling is obvious, it will always require obedience.

Duck, Dodge and Run

Some Pathfinders already know what God is calling them to do, but for some reason, oftentimes because of fear, they decide to run the opposite direction of what God told them to do. Such is the case in Jonah 1. The challenge with being a runner is that your life will likely never be fully settled until you answer God's call. The Lord will sometimes plant seeds in us as children or teenagers to want to pursue a certain field or career. It may be easy to doubt a childhood dream, but if it is still inside you some twenty, thirty or fifty years later, then you need to seek the Lord through prayer immediately and ask Him if He wants you to do something about that dream that is still there.

The Sleeping Giant

The Lord will sometimes place Pathfinders in a job or position for years before He awakens the purpose associated with that role. If you have volunteered with an organization or worked for a company for a long time but are sensing that God may want you to do something different, you may be on to something. The Holy Spirit may be awakening you to your purpose exactly where you are. Esther had a similar experience. It wasn't until her Uncle Mordecai prompted her to consider that maybe she became Queen to save her people that Esther began to embrace her purpose for the position she already occupied (Esther 4:14).

Rise to the Occasion

Many Pathfinders will simply emerge into their purpose, seemingly out of nowhere. They will be going along with their life until one day, the Lord reveals His assignment. The beloved Mary, the mother of Jesus, was like that. She was young and engaged to be married when an Angel of the Lord came to her and told her she was going to have a baby soon. We know that Mary was highly favored by

God. Scripture does not tell us why she stood out from the crowd of women, but she had to have reverence for the Lord and behavior that somehow pleased God to be chosen as God's Baby Mama. While Mary's purpose emerged unexpectedly, it had substance and impact because of the quality of her relationship with God. Luke 1:46-55, gives us an indication of Mary's reverence for God and her level of understanding of His nature.

Spoiler Alert

So, the funny thing is that we all have the same purpose. How and when our purpose is revealed is a truly individual experience, but what our purpose is, has a universal appeal.

I am sure many of us have wondered and asked repeatedly for years, "What is my life purpose? What is my life purpose?" As usual, Scripture gives the answer. God is cool like that.

Our purpose is to fulfill what is often referred to as, the Great Commission.

Therefore, go and make disciples of all the nations baptizing them in the name of the Father and the Son and the Holy Spirit. Matthew 28:19

Now, let's be honest here. When we think about the Great Commission, some of our minds instantly take a transatlantic voyage. When we think about making disciples, thoughts of serving as a missionary in a third world country usually come up for me. Now, in full disclosure, I'm a bonafide city girl. The idea of living somewhere without indoor plumbing and air conditioning, feels like a cross too big for me to bear! And while the sacrificial lifestyles many missionaries graciously endure to share the gospel, do come to mind, the fact of the matter is, most of us will not have the capability, opportunity or calling to serve in a third world country.

However, as a Pathfinder, your purpose is still rooted in fulfilling this wonderful, life-giving command. Before you hit the abort button on this mission, you should know that your unique purpose is determined by how God chooses to use all your life experiences, gifts, talents and personal qualities to define your life purpose.

Your assignment is dispatched when God brings all of who you are together in this sort of lightbulb, "aha" moment where you say, "Wow, this is why x, y, and z happened in my life. I now know what I am supposed to do."

Because we all have an assignment, there will be a moment or series of experiences where it will become very clear how God will uniquely use you to draw others to Him through many factors: your story, service, career, life season and talents. Our ultimate purpose is to give God glory, but the way that we accomplish that is unique and specific to each of us as individuals.

Ta-da! Your life purpose is now defined, and this is when the fun really begins.

How you carry out or execute your purpose is where the quest gets interesting. Ironically, you have already been on the path to purpose from the day that you were born. God has used circumstances or allowed certain situations to happen in your life. We already know this based on our previous studies.

As a result, God has used those experiences to shape, mold and inform who you are. When the time is right, God will reveal his assignment for you and it will be specifically yours. There will also be people who are connected to and depending on you to carry out your assignment.

That is why it is so important that we learn to recognize the phases of the Life Purpose Map. That is why we must be expert Pathfinders because if we're not careful, we may miss our assignment.

There are a ton of influencers and authors who instruct you to find your passion and pursue it, but I believe that is only half the equation. It is not enough to simply know what you are passionate about without the proper context. The critical link is knowing what you're passionate about and combining that with an understanding of our ultimate purpose on earth - to bring God glory and draw others to Him.

Compass Points

Key learning and reflection points from this chapter.

1. God is not confined to a method, system or formula. He will reveal your purpose in a way that is consistent with His character and unique to you.

2. As Believers, we all share the universal purpose of helping to bring others to Christ. The exact way or avenue that we accomplish this purpose will be unique to our life experiences and who God created us to be.

3. Your path to purpose began the day you were born. Our awareness of or awakening to our purpose, is what we are seeking.

Coaching and Discovery Questions

1. How are you sensing that the Holy Spirit is speaking to you about your purpose?

   _____

   _____

   _____

2. What could you do to have a more open mindset and posture about your calling?

   _____

   _____

   _____

3. How do you feel about your purpose being associated with fulfilling the Great Commission?

   _____

   _____

   _____

Reflections

_____

_____

_____

_____

_____

_____

_____

_____

_____

_____

_____

_____

Pathfinder Phase 4

Pursue

We must quickly carry out
the tasks assigned us by the
one who sent us...

John 9:4

CHAPTER 8

PURSUE WITHOUT FORCE

And David inquired of the LORD, "Shall I pursue
after this band? Shall I overtake them?" He answered
him, "Pursue, for you shall surely overtake and shall
surely rescue." 1 Samuel 30:8 ESV

How God chooses to reveal and make known how He wants to use you, is entirely up to Him. I am a planner by nature. As a young girl, on Sundays, I would plan my school wardrobe for the entire upcoming week. Professionally, I thrive on developing strategies for my consulting and coaching clients, and in my personal life, I enjoy creating to-do lists to manage family activities and home improvement projects. I think you get the idea.

Developing a vision, strategy and action plan is part of my DNA. I feel like I am *always* thinking, and sometimes wish I could just turn my brain off, but that's how I am wired. I don't say this to brag. I say this to highlight the significance of my point.

During this beautiful and perfectly designed path to your purpose, there are some things to watch out for. And it may go against your very nature to heed my warnings, but this is important.

Pathfinder Tip: Pursue God's plan but submit to His timing and His ways. Be careful to observe and seek clarity about each step of your journey.

As strong, independent women, learning to surrender to God's will and timing may be one of *the* most difficult lessons we have to learn along the path to our purpose. While, thankfully, not all of us are extreme planners, there is a tendency for us women to bear much of the responsibility of multi-tasking to balance all facets of our lives and the many hats we wear.

We often start at an early age, from organizing a min-ute-by-minute itinerary for play dates to coordinating the next Girls' Night Out with our friends. We have important life milestones we want to achieve by a certain age. We plan all the time. Unfortunately, this hardwired desire to strategize and project manage our lives is the antithesis of walking by faith, especially when we hold our desires and plans tightly.

While God is Sovereign, and His Will will always be done, the way we think and behave can interfere with God's *perfect* will manifesting in our life.

Don't copy the behavior and customs of this world, but let God transform you into a new person by changing the way you think. Then you will learn to know God's will for you, which is good and pleasing and perfect. (Romans 12:2)

In the first part of this verse, we find a conditional statement. We are warned that we should not behave like the world. In order to not act like the world, we have to allow God to change us into a new person by changing the way we think. Some of us focus on trying to change the outward appearance of our lives. Romans 12 clearly tells us that it is the refining and transformative relationship with the Lord that enables us to shift our mindset. When our minds adjust, our behavior, habits, and attitudes will follow.

As our mind is transformed by God, we are then able to learn God's will for our lives. I love how the King James translation states this passage, "transformed by the renewing of your mind, that ye may prove what is that good, and acceptable, and perfect, will of God."

Here, it is clearer to see that there are distinct types of God's will. Some characterize this concept as God's permissive will versus His perfect will. Oswald Chambers states, "Always make a distinction between God's perfect will and His permissive will, which He uses to accomplish His divine purpose for our lives. God's perfect will is unchangeable. It is with His permissive will or the various things that He allows into our lives, that we must wrestle before Him. It is our reaction to these things allowed by His permissive will that enables us to come to the point of seeing His perfect will for us" (Chambers, 2018).

One of your great challenges along the path to purpose will be your ability to navigate knowing, with certainty, what God may allow or permit you to do and what His perfect will is. In case you are a little skeptical, let's look at some women in the Bible who appeared to straddle the line between the permissive and perfect will of God.

Eve

The mother of us all, Eve truly had the perfect husband, perfect house, and perfect life. She is the purest example of what it looks like to walk in God's perfect will, until that dreaded day when she developed her own plan. She decided that the forbidden fruit looked appealing, and despite God's perfect instruction, she ate the fruit and gave it to her husband. After the Fall, we know that Adam and Eve, and all of us who follow, live in some level of God's permissive will (Genesis 3:6).

Sarah

This woman and her husband, Abraham, learned about their purpose during a VIP visit from an Angel of the Lord. Sarah laughed at the visitor when he told her that she would conceive a son. After all, she and her husband were well beyond the child-bearing age, and they had not been able to conceive prior in life. One important aspect of the path to purpose is that just because God reveals what He will do in your life, does not mean He wants you to execute it immediately. Sarah and Abraham learned this lesson the hard way. After becoming impatient with waiting for God's plans to be fulfilled, Sarah took matters into her own hands. Abraham received an heir, but not from Sarah, and to this day, conflict in the Middle East continues because of one act of impatience and forcing a version of God's plan to come to fruition before it is time (Genesis 18:1-15).

Rebekah

As parents or future parents, we often have great aspirations and hopes for our children. We see their glorious potential long before they do. We recognize their natural gifting and talents. We connect with their personalities and quirks in a way only a mother can. Rebeca was like many of us. The mother of twin sons, Esau and Jacob, Rebekah allowed her dreams and desires for one son to rule her actions. Bucking Jewish tradition, she wanted her youngest son, Jacob, to receive the special blessing of birthright from his father which would allow him to inherit the rights and privileges of his father's position. Rebeca, with Jacob in cahoots, devised an intricate plan of deception to ensure her plan was fulfilled. For Bible scholars, it may be easy to respond to this scenario with a shrug of the shoulders and a dismissive response of, "Well, God foretold there would be two nations and conflict between the sons." We should be very careful here. While Rebekah and Jacob got what they wanted through their dubious plan, and God's purpose ultimately prevailed, it is important to note that their actions caused a bitter rift between twin brothers (Genesis 27:34-40).

In my own journey toward purpose, there have been many highs, lows and defining moments. As my relationship with the Lord has grown, I am able to more clearly recognize His fingerprints on my life. During the moment, it can be easy to overlook the significance of what God has done in our lives. That's why I am a big fan of journaling and documenting key milestones in your spiritual walk.

When I look at the night sky and see the work of your fingers—the moon and the stars you set in place—what are mere mortals that you should think about them, human beings that you should care for them? Psalms 8:3-4

By keeping a record of insights, ideas, truths, and guidance from the Lord, we can sharpen our spiritual vision. Early in my walk with the Lord, I would often struggle with discernment and would ask the Lord, "Is this You or is it me?" In other words, if I would have an idea about something, I would struggle to know if I should act on it for fear of being out of the will of God. Any form of fear can be paralyzing if we allow it, especially fear of missing what God would have us do in a situation.

Another reason why it is a good idea to capture the movement and miracles of God is that we can refer to our journal when we are discouraged. I love flipping through the pages of my journal written years ago. Sometimes, I would simply journal about my feelings and literally write my prayers to the Lord. So, it's not always about writing down the "big stuff" the Lord has done for us. Looking back and reading about the dark and painful periods are powerful because I now have the perspective of, "Wow, I survived. The Lord brought me through." On a particular date, many years ago, or even last week, I felt a certain way. At the time I wrote in my journal, the situation was not resolved, but my mere survival is proof of God's grace!

Compass Points

Key learning and reflection points from this chapter.

1. We must be aware that it's possible to be in God's will, but not necessarily His perfect will.

2. Submitting to God's plans and His timing are essential to walking in His will.

3. Keep a record of major "It Had to Be God" milestones in your life. Over time, you will create a collection of insights and wisdom gained, which will help you better identify how He is leading you.

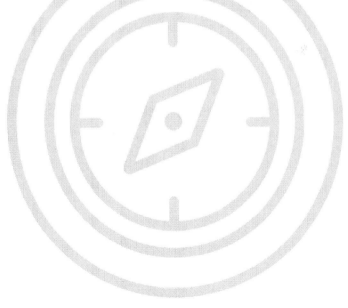

Coaching and Discovery Questions

1. When it comes to surrendering to the will of God, which of the women we explored on the previous pages do you identify with most? Why?

_____

_____

_____

2. What are some examples of significant spiritual mile-stones – moments when you could clearly see God operating in your life?

_____

_____

_____

3. As you look back, what is the Holy Spirit reminding you of as you think about how God's Presence has been in your life?

_____

_____

_____

Reflections

CHAPTER 9

SURVIVAL GUIDE

I am as strong now as I was when Moses sent me on that journey, and I can still travel and fight as well as I could then. Joshua 14:11

There are always those ladies who are down for whatever may come. They are the girls who all you have to do is say the word, and they are ready to roll. They have your back and ask no questions.

We all need a little of that spunk and grit on the path to purpose, as long as it's balanced with grace and submission to the Lord. For all my girls who are ready and in position, this chapter is for you.

Here, you will find some practical guidance about how to pursue your purpose while avoiding some common mistakes. Once the Lord reveals your purpose, it is time to move. In fact, you will likely come to know your purpose only after you act on a prompting by the Holy Spirit.

We have already discussed the importance of pursuing purpose without forcing it to fit our mold. God may allow it for a period of time, but there will be consequences if you do not fully surrender your plans and will to Him.

Below are my seven Pathfinder survival tips. Refer to these whenever you feel stuck or confused.

#1 Become familiar with how the Holy Spirit speaks to you. Your prayer and devotional life are so critical to developing spiritually, and without a strong foundation of communicating on a regular basis with the Lord, you will not be able to discern His voice. We must practice active listening.

#2 Know that fasting may be required at times. As I have mentioned before, there will be dark periods on the path to purpose where it feels like you are not hearing anything from the Lord. Fasting is an incredible spiritual practice of deep submission to the Lord. As we deprive our tummies, our hearts become more sensitive to the Holy Spirit. A great resource for fasting newbies is a book simply titled, *Fasting* by Jentezen Franklin. I highly recommend it and be sure to check with your doctor before fasting food.

#3 Every vision is not for right now. This Pathfinder truth can be a tough pill to swallow. As you mature spiritually, the Lord may reveal to you glimpses of His vision for your life, and oh, how remarkable it is to receive such a gift from Him! If the Holy Spirit reveals to you an idea, vision or new concept, before you act on it, be sure to ask the Lord to clarify when He wants you to pursue.

#4 Learn to embrace the shakes. Have you ever experienced muscle fatigue during a workout? It's where your muscle quivers and shakes from exertion and being pushed to its limits. You will experience similar, but spiritual, shaking on the path to purpose. Through real and tangible life situations, God will allow your faith to be tested for what feels like its final limits. Learn to embrace these faith-stretching seasons by giving thanks.

#5 Hardship does not mean you made a mistake. If you start to pursue what you believe God has asked you to do, and you meet resistance or even what appears to be a failure, please do not lose heart. Sometimes, we can inadvertently slip into our old tendencies of trying to control the situation based on what we want or know. This can cause us to veer off the path and not realize it until we take an ugly tumble. It will be okay. Just dust yourself off and get back to seeking the Lord.

#6 Checkmate, it's your move. If you get to a point where you feel like you are doing everything "right" but still nothing is changing, then it's a good time to check back in with the Lord and ask Him to clarify His original instructions. You may have missed a detail or even ignored doing something really simple. There is no sugarcoating it, you are in disobedience and you must fix it as quickly as possible by following His original direction to you.

#7 Stop the merry-go-round madness. If a topic, idea, person or venture keeps coming to your attention, especially unsolicited, you need to pay attention. In His great mercy, God will often give us multiple chances to see what He has been trying to tell us. Avoid dismissing what God could be bringing into your life to guide you toward your purpose. Remember that God's ways are not like ours, so the very person or thing we are ignoring or dismissing, could be an integral part of your path to purpose.

Compass Points

Key learning and reflection points from this chapter.

1. We know that faith without works is not really faith. Walking in our purpose requires action.

2. When you feel stuck in life, use the Seven Pathfinder Survival Tips to help you find your way.

3. Remember that God is never the author of confusion!

Coaching and Discovery Questions

1. In what ways have you recognized the Holy Spirit speaking to you?

    _____

    _____

    _____

2. How do you know when you are being led to fast?

    _____

    _____

    _____

3. What goals, visions, desires or dreams has the Holy Spirit put on your heart? Be sure to write them down.

    _____

    _____

    _____

4. In what ways could you get discernment about whether the Lord wants you to be still or take action in a situation?

_____

_____

_____

5. How do you handle major setbacks or mistakes? Is there anything you need to forgive yourself for?

_____

_____

_____

6. What instruction or action do you feel the Lord has already given you? What have you done in this area?

_____

_____

_____

7. What situations, ideas or topics seem to be recurring themes in your life?

_____

_____

_____

Reflections

_____

_____

_____

_____

_____

_____

_____

_____

_____

_____

_____

_____

Pathfinder Phase 5

Flourish

All Scripture is inspired by God and is useful to teach us what is true and to make us realize what is wrong in our lives. It corrects us when we are wrong and teaches us to do what is right. God uses it to prepare and equip his people to do every good work.

2 Timothy 3:16-17

CHAPTER 10

PURPOSE NOT PERFECTION

Our people must learn to do good by meeting the urgent
needs of others; then they will not be unproductive.
Titus 3:14

For Pathfinders who have discovered their calling, you have reached the stage on the Life Purpose Map where it is time to embrace it, own it and walk fully in it. While your initial steps within your purpose may feel awkward in the beginning – like a newly born deer taking its first steps – don't worry, you will get stronger as long as you keep moving forward.

The beauty of walking in purpose is that you will gain momentum with each step of obedience you take. Your purpose journey is not about perfection. There will be hiccups along the way, but there will be benefits to experiencing those bumps and dips.

We can rejoice, too, when we run into problems and trials, for we know that they help us develop endurance. And endurance develops strength of character, and character strengthens our confident hope of salvation. And this hope will not lead to disappointment. For we know how dearly God loves us because he has given us the Holy Spirit to fill our hearts with his love. Romans 5:3-5

To flourish as we walk in our purpose may seem like a misnomer for experienced Pathfinders. The reality is that those of us on the path to purpose will experience bitter struggles, spiritual warfare and periods of what feels like silence from the Lord. There will be times when worry, anxiety and unbelief are so thick and heavy, we will have to muster all our strength and hope to wear a garment of praise even when we don't feel like it (Isaiah 61:3).

The path to purpose has many dark shadows along the way, but it also has brilliantly shining rays of hope, joy and character-building resilience. You will come to know that you are capable of more than you thought. You will come to know that our God is truly greater than any other god, any battle we face or obstacle that tries to trip us and make us fall off His path.

My dear Pathfinder, please know that His hand is always there. His eye is always upon you. We serve a God who is familiar with and sensitive to what we feel (Hebrews 4:15). He is not a cold statue or shapeless aura of lights.

Sustain the Momentum

There are some key behaviors and steps you will want to maintain in order to truly flourish in your purpose. If we are not careful, we can start walking in purpose using our head and not our spirit. If you maintain these behaviors, you will be more likely to sustain God's Presence and movement in your life.

1. Keep your relationship with the Lord as your number one priority. Your purpose should not become an idol to you (Deuteronomy 6:5).

2. Be spiritually authentic, disciplined and consistent. Avoid a worldly lifestyle and focus on material things (Luke 8:14). Fasting is a great way to improve spiritual discipline.

3. Godly accountability in a loving community is crucial (Hebrews 10:25). Surround yourself with other Pathfinders. Connect with us online through the Cubicles & Christ Community on Facebook.

4. Pathfinders follow the flow of purpose. Scripture constantly points to a divine cycle: believe, receive, give, repeat. What we receive from the Lord should not be hoarded for ourselves (Proverbs 11:24-25).

5. Use basic goal-setting principles and apply them toward your walk with the Lord. Set aside time at least annually to spend "strategic" time with the Lord. Go on retreats to have quiet time with the Lord so that you can hear from Him, distraction-free. Write down what you hear (Habakkuk 2:2).

Our purpose will always be tied to how God chooses to use us to fulfill the Great Commission - to share the good news of Jesus Christ. Our purpose, if we're truly being spiritually authentic, will never be one that is self-serving, or designed to give us fame just for the sake of celebrity status.

The Word of God says that we should not despise humble beginnings, and so yes, there are times when God will exalt some of His servants, but the platform is used to reach more lives and draw more people to Him (Zechariah 4:10).

I think one of the misperceptions for those of us seeking our purpose is that it's about finding a new job or career. In and of itself, our purpose is not about a job or career change.

Sometimes, once our purpose has been identified, we will go through a career change, but sometimes God wants to use us in our current jobs, schools or volunteer activities. When we are awakened to our purpose in whatever environment He has us operating in, that is when we have truly become spiritually authentic. Philippians 1:6, tells us that God will finish the good work He started in us and that my dear Pathfinder, is truly good news.

Compass Points

Key learning and reflection points from this chapter.

1. Your journey to purpose is not about perfection. There will be mistakes along the way, but there will be benefits to experiencing those bumps and bruises.

2. Consistency is key. Sustain the momentum of God operating in your life by prioritizing your relationship with Him.

3. Baby steps are okay and part of the process. Avoid wanting to wear your big girl shoes too soon.

Coaching and Discovery Questions

1. What has the Holy Spirit been saying to you as you read this book?

_____

_____

_____

2. Who in your close circle provides you with Biblical counsel, wisdom, and advice on a regular basis?

_____

_____

_____

3. Who in your life could become a spiritual coach or mentor to you?

_____

_____

_____

4. Who are you providing godly counsel, wisdom, and advice to on a regular basis?

_____

_____

_____

Reflections

_____

_____

_____

_____

_____

_____

_____

_____

_____

_____

_____

_____

_____

CHAPTER 11

CLOSING REMARKS

Now may the God of peace—who brought up from the
dead our Lord Jesus, the great Shepherd of the sheep,
and ratified an eternal covenant with his blood—may
he equip you with all you need for doing his will. May
he produce in you,[c] through the power of Jesus Christ,
every good thing that is pleasing to him. All glory to him
forever and ever! Amen.
Hebrews 13:20-21

Before we pray, it is important to highlight that the contents of this book carry an important prerequisite. In school, we know that there are certain classes that require you to take foundational classes before you can register for more advanced curriculum. In some ways, *EMERGE!* is similar.

Before any of us can walk in God's purpose for our life, we must first be 100 percent sure that we are in a personal relationship with Jesus Christ, and that we have accepted Him as our Lord and Savior. If there is any uncertainty or hesitation in your mind about your salvation status, I want to encourage you to become absolutely certain right now. It's so easy, and the Father is always waiting for us with open and loving arms.

Romans 10:9-10 provides straightforward guidance on what is required for salvation. Simply put, we must say that Jesus is Lord with our mouths and we must believe in our heart that God raised Him from the dead. That's all it takes, and this simple step is the number one most important step for every Pathfinder.

If you are unsure about how you should pray for salvation, consider this prayer by Dr. Ray Pritchard.

> *Lord Jesus, for too long I've kept you out of my life. I know that I am a sinner and that I cannot save myself. No longer will I close the door when I hear you knocking. By faith I gratefully receive your gift of salvation. I am ready to trust you as my Lord and Savior. Thank you, Lord Jesus, for coming to earth. I believe you are the Son of God who died*

on the cross for my sins and rose from the dead on the third day. Thank you for bearing my sins and giving me the gift of eternal life. I believe your words are true. Come into my heart, Lord Jesus, and be my Savior. Amen. (Crosswalk Editorial Staff, 2018)

Closing Prayer

Gracious and Sovereign Lord,

We come to you now thanking you for the wonderful plans and purposes that you have for each of us (Jeremiah 29:11). Thank you, Lord that your purposes will prevail and stand (Proverbs 19:21). No tactic or maneuver by the enemy can prevent us from victory (Isaiah 54:17)!

We ask you, Dear Lord, to give us wisdom, insight, and discernment about where you are leading us and what action you would have us to take. Also, Lord, please show us when you want us to take those actions.

Search our hearts and help us to know any area that is unlike you and show us where we need to submit further to your Light and your Ways (Psalms 139:24-25).

Bring us further into the understanding of your knowledge and Truth. Thank you for ordering our steps and leading us on a path of righteousness for your name's sake (Psalms 119:139).

Please bless the work of our hands, Almighty Father, and enlarge our territories as you see fit (Psalms 90:17). Help us to be good stewards and managers of your resources and the gifts and talents you have given us.

We thank you in advance for all that you are doing in our lives. We thank you for your faithfulness, and we thank you, Lord, that you will never leave us or forsake us.

In your Holy and Righteous Name, we pray, Amen.

CLOSING REMARKS

_____

_____

_____

_____

_____

_____

_____

_____

_____

_____

_____

_____

_____

MEET THE AUTHOR

Kelley believes we all have a purpose, and she is on a mission to encourage and empower others to align their passion with their purpose to impact the world and God's Kingdom.

Her career spans more than 20 years in corporate America, where she received many accolades and rose to become one of just a few Black female vice presidents in a Fortune 500 company.

Today, she is CEO of a strategy consulting and executive coaching firm. She is host of the popular *Cubicles & Christ* podcast available on Apple Podcast, Spotify, Google Play, and Stitcher.

A graduate of Texas Woman's University and a Hogan certified executive coach, she is most proud of her roles as a wife, mom, and servant in ministry.

 @iamkelleyjohnson

LET'S CONNECT!

Kelley is a sought-after speaker and has engaged audiences of all sizes at churches, professional associations, universities and major corporations. Please visit **iamkelleyjohnson.com** for more information.

BOOK KELLEY FOR YOUR EVENT!

✉ INFO@IAMKELLEYJOHNSON.COM

Catch the latest episodes on Apple Podcasts, Google Play, Spotify and Stitcher.

REFERENCES

Benner, J. (2018, August 18). *Ancient Hebrew Research Center*. Retrieved from The Ancient Hebrew Alphabet: http://www.ancient-hebrew.org/alphabet_letters_aleph.html

Benson, R. J. (2018, August 21). *Benson Commentary on the Old and New Testaments*. Retrieved from Bible Hub: https://biblehub.com/commentaries/benson/psalms/119.htm

Chambers, O. (2018, August 8). *Wrestling Before God*. Retrieved from My Utmost for His Highest: https://utmost.org/wrestling-before-god/

Crosswalk Editorial Staff. (2018, October 22). *The Sinner's Prayer - 4 Examples for Salvation*. Retrieved from Crosswalk: https://www.crosswalk.com/faith/prayer/prayers/the-sinners-prayer-4-examples.html

Made in the USA
Columbia, SC
16 December 2018